MW00441591

"I only wish MESSAGES from God had been published before starting out on my own journey to success. Lynn has made it her purpose in life to help others succeed in their goals. The passage in her book, 'You can have anything you want, surrender to the possibilities,' sums it all up for me. Valuable reading."

WILLIAM RIEAD
Chairman and CEO, CinemaWest Corporation

"Like Rudyard Kipling's 'If,' these insightful passages chronicle every person's life history. Where you have been, where you are now and where you are capable of going. These are the building blocks to a deeper and more meaningful life. You'll want to read them again and again."

CHARLES SHEFFIELD
Chairman, U.S. Design and Construction Corp.

"There's nothing limited or impossible with Lynn Marks, and to prove it she's telling us all about the powerful MESSAGES from God. Not only will it awaken your spirit, this book will jump-start it."

TOM HARKEN
Author of *THE MILLIONAIRE'S SECRET*

"MESSAGES from God is both practical and inspirational. Lynn's insights can challenge us all from the inside out."

STEPHANIE FARWIG
16 Year LPGA Tour Veteran

"MESSAGES from God is a call to action for leaders to stay on their true path to success."

BILL ROGERS
President, World Entrepreneur Society

Messages from God

365 Simple Truths for Success

LYNN S. MARKS

◖◗ Golden Halo Productions

P. O. Box 22545, Houston, TX 77227

Publisher's Cataloging-in-Publication Data

Marks, Lynn S.
   Messages from God: 365 simple truths for success /
Lynn S. Marks. -- 1st ed.
   p.cm.
   ISBN: 1-888783-31-1

   1. Success in business--Religious aspects--
Quotations, maxims, etc. 2. Conduct of life--
Quotations, maxims, etc. 3. Wealth--Psychological
aspects--Quotations, maxims, etc. 4. Maxims,
American. I. Title

   HF5386.M37 1999   650.1
                                QBI98-1684

Printed in Hong Kong by Creative Printing Limited.

Printed on acid-free paper.

10 9 8 7 6 5 4 3 2

A PORTION OF THE AUTHOR'S PROCEEDS FROM THIS BOOK WILL GO TO THE
NONPROFIT BIG BROTHERS BIG SISTERS OF AMERICA.

DEDICATION

With love and gratitude to God
whose wisdom continuously
flows through me
and touches others to be all
who they are meant to be.

And, to Mom, Ana "Bonnie" Marks,
whose life, lessons and love have been
my teacher.

CONTENTS

Acknowledgements

I AM FILLED WITH LOVE AND GRATITUDE
for all of my personal angels whose love and
support are a constant inspiration:

Alice Sweet, a brilliant therapist whose illus-
trations grace this book, for asking "Do you
know the power of what you do?" and then
typing up the messages that touched her and
dubbing them "Perfect Pearls of Wisdom by
the Quotable Coach."

My loving family, Dave Allen, my husband,
and Angel, my puppy, for your unwavering,
unconditional love.

My clients, for entrusting me with your lives

and your work and being a constant source of inspiration.

The Friends of Lynn for your commitment to personal growth while supporting my work by attending my monthly luncheons, seminars and retreats.

Susan Daniels, my dear friend and editor, for always being there with your ever deep belief in me, my mission and my work.

Sydney Seaward, for your friendship, courage and spirituality to a vision that is beyond limitations.

Rohan Kulkarni, my technology point man and computer wizard, for coming to my rescue so many times.

And my production and marketing team, including Sheryn Hara, Suzy Morris, Bob Orkand and Lina Lou for understanding and supporting the vision of this book.

OREWORD

by Sydney Seaward
Subject of **Lifetime**'s *"Intimate Portrait"*

THIS BOOK IS ABOUT PEOPLE. IT IS about people who care enough about life to live it to the greatest extent they can — in all the splendor and beauty that has externally been up for grabs — all for us, just for the taking.

One day I received a telephone call from Lynn Marks to be on a national radio show as her guest. At that unexpected moment, I had no idea how my life was about to change or how big a part Lynn Marks was to play in it.

Messages from God: 365 Simple Truths for Success will change your life as that seemingly chance telephone call changed mine — if you are open to change.

This book is for you, if you want to change for the better; if you choose to embrace life; if you are ready to embrace life; and if you can face living the best way you can possibly live.

Lynn Marks and her ideas are hard to label. She is more than just a speaker. She is more than just a motivator. She is more than just a unique kind of coach. And, she is more than *only* an extremely gifted woman. Lynn Marks is alive, in every sense of the word. She truly lives and shows others how to do the same. Lynn lives and shares with us all the beautiful and powerful poetry and potential in life. Lynn is here on this earth for one simple purpose: To make our lives better. How could we possibly pass up such an opportunity to grab our greatest potential? I couldn't.

It is now your choice to grasp, embrace and cherish it--to learn how to make yourself the best you can possibly be, with Lynn's help. *Messages from God: 365 Simple Truths for Success* is simply a shortcut to doing that. This is now your choice and chance to join her in the wondrous adventure each of us has a right to call life.

Welcome and enjoy as I have.

*I*NTRODUCTION

IMAGINE HAVING YOUR LIFE'S PURPOSE achieved and your dreams fulfilled. There is a way.

If you are ready, the extraordinary wisdom that follows will show you how to create the life you seek, the life you deserve.

Early in my career during a regular coaching call, a client posed a question for which I am eternally grateful: "Do you know the power of what you do?"

Not clear what she meant, I asked rather innocently, "What?"

She said, "You speak in messages that change lives."

Still not conscious of the significance of her insight or the depth of my being, I said

*I*t's about communicating truths.

rather feebly, "Yes, I know I speak in messages."

Undaunted, she proceeded to type the messages from our meetings that touched her and dubbed them "Perfect Pearls of Wisdom."

At the time, I was somewhat embarrassed. Like many artists, my gift came naturally to me. The words, the messages, just flowed through me in conversational style. And then, like a laser, the messages touched people. Once inspired, most dramatically changed and improved their lives. I took this as normal. After all, my life's purpose is to assist people to be all they are meant to be.

That was some five years ago. I dabbled with the idea of collecting the messages and creating this book. Ultimately, I let it go and enjoyed my clients and my service while deepening my abilities. And then my clients and friends asked for my products. I listened. It was time.

Once I embraced the concept that the

contents of a book had been given to me for a reason, it came together very quickly. And then, not much happened. I asked God why the book wasn't working and was told that I had the wrong title. I asked what was the right title and was told *Messages from God*.

Admittedly, I was rather resistant. For most of the week, I went through a myriad of thoughts, emotions and questions. Who am I to bring forth such a title? What will people think? Am I ready for those who will accuse me of blasphemy, of being a disciple or new age? Will this affect business?

And then I seemed to come out of the storm. I now knew, who am I *not* to bring forth these powerful, life-changing messages?

After all, I have been sharing these messages coaching clients for years and more recently with speaking audiences. Clients and audiences alike repeatedly acknowledge their universal appeal and impact.

I know that sharing these experiences and messages will offend some. Call it intuition,

*I*t's never too
late to be
everything
you are meant
to be.

instinct, gut feelings, God voice, higher knowing, spirit — it does not matter. It is about communicating truths.

These simple messages awaken people's spirits. Whether heard or read, when touched, people know their truth. They say they were transformed. They were empowered. It was as if I were speaking only to them.

For many, their lives dramatically changed — their attitudes, behaviors, friends, lifestyles, and careers. They moved from being victims to becoming leaders of their own destiny; from suffering, tolerating and struggling to ease, peace and abundance; and from trying hard and proving that they were good enough to being their perfect gift. They shifted from a life filled with "incompletions" to a life of integrity.

Many refer to these words as my words and acknowledge me for changing their lives. I have come to know and accept that I am a messenger, one of many, who carries God's words for those who are ready. Much like that expression, "When the student is ready, the teacher will appear."

Messages from God will remind you of your strength, goodness and truth. These messages are for you if you are ready to live your life — personally and professionally — at the highest level. These messages are for you if you are ready to live the life you deserve. It's your choice.

It's never too late to be everything you are meant to be.

May you experience the miracles of *Messages from God*. May they touch your heart and awaken your spirit.

Lynn S. Marks
Houston, Texas
Thanksgiving 1998

$\mathscr{A}$ NOTE FROM THE AUTHOR

THIS BOOK IS A COMPILATION OF LIFE-transforming messages. If you will allow these God-given messages to lead you, a whole new and higher level of living will become available to you — a life of limitless possibilities.

For best results, I request that you make it a lifelong habit to read these messages every day. Read them knowing you are already perfect and getting better and better.

Read them as you would a menu at a restaurant. Look down the list, scan the pages. Note where your eyes are naturally drawn, then stop. There is no need to read any further that day. This is your personal message for the day.

You may find your mind saying things like: "No. That can't be. It's not possible." Often we

There is
great wisdom in
nothingness.

resist that which makes us whole.

There is great wisdom in nothingness. You need do nothing with these messages. Your consciousness will take in the message and automatically start rearranging itself to support your new awareness.

Do not be disturbed if you are drawn to the same message again and again throughout the days, weeks, months, and years to come.

Each time you refocus on the message, your consciousness is raised to the next level. This heightened awareness increases your personal standards. And, as if by magic, those around you simultaneously increase their standards as well or self-select out of your community.

They say the eyes are the window of the soul. Trust them. They know.

These messages will transform your life — personally and professionally — if you will allow them.

MESSAGES from God

365 Simple Truths for Success

There are many choices,
but only one path.

Life is too great
to let anyone or anything
hold you back
from personal success.
It is your choice.

*A*nticipation
drains your personal power.

*I*n your heart
you know what's right.
Give yourself permission to
feel it, say it, do it, be it.

$\mathcal{B}$elieve in possibilities
— always.

$\mathcal{Y}$ou can have anything
that you want. Live, breathe
and believe with your heart,
not your head.

*B*e positive.
Come from love
and compassion,
not judgment and criticism.

*A*ttitude is power
– positive or negative.
It's your choice.

*A*uthentic living takes effort,
not struggle.

*R*isk being all you are
meant to be — regardless
of what others
think or say.

*T*ell people
what you want.
Allow the human angels
to provide for you.

*F*ace your anger.
Forgive yourself,
forgive others.
Feel your love grow.

The only thing that gets
in your way of receiving
life's goodness is you.
Change your beliefs,
upgrade your standards.

The world reflects your
attitude toward it
– make it love.

$\mathcal{E}$mbrace your divine being.
Come from love,
not superiority.

$\mathcal{Y}$ou don't have to do it all
to have it all.

Shift from serving your self
to serving humanity.
Infinite abundance
is yours.

Be grateful. See and feel
the abundance all
around you.

Clutter blocks
the passageway
to abundance.
Clear your incompletions.

Anything you can conceive
you can achieve.

Achieve your heart's
desires through
quiet contemplation,
not busyness and worry.

You can do anything you
want. You just don't have
to do it all yourself.

*R*eal wealth is measured
by the quality of your
community and friends.

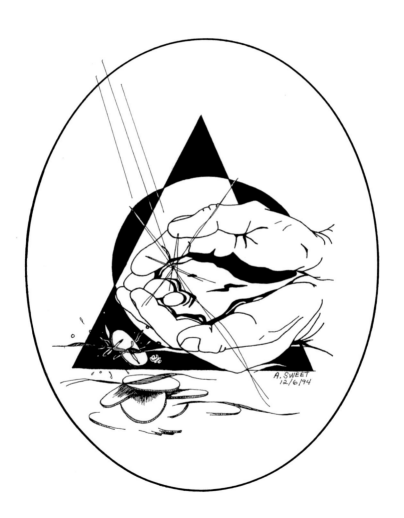

A. SWEET
12/6/94

You are in the right place
when life is more fun
than work.

Get your heart and soul
behind your goals.

*A*ttachments drain your
health, wealth and
happiness.

*A*ttaining personal
success is continuously
living your life
from choice.

*D*on't be the expert,
be yourself.

*D*are to be who you are.
Be your gift.

$\mathcal{Y}$ou can't be there for
others unless you are there
for yourself — first.

$\mathcal{F}$ully express
who you are.
Be tolerant-free.

*E*xpand your beliefs,
expand your possibilities.

*W*hen you feel it,
speak it.

Accept,
do not judge and
move on.

Be fully conscious.
Be aware of the truth within
and live it daily.

*M*editate, commune,
listen in quietness.
Heighten your awareness
of the truth within.

*W*hen your heart speaks,
act. And ACT now.

What is meant to be, is.

Stop trying to
figure it out.
Ask God.

You can do anything.
Turn your fears over to
God and go forth freely.

The present flows perfectly
when you focus on the now.

*R*elease your need to
know *why*.
Flow with life's force.

*T*he future is now.

*E*xpress your gifts fully.
Surround yourself with
those who support and
encourage your talents.

*G*race comes to those who
know they deserve it.
Believe.

$\mathcal{B}$e willing to feel again
like that happy little child
in the sandbox.

$\mathcal{H}$onor yourself first.
Others will benefit too.

*H*onor yourself first
in all that you say and do.

*L*ife is good;
all else is an illusion.

*I*mpossibilities are
possibilities waiting for
imagination and will.

*B*elieve the incredible,
not the logical.

*W*ant more, need less.

*B*e bold.
Visualize receiving
50 percent more than you
think you can or should.

*I*nfinite abundance and
fulfillment come from
realizing God's will,
not yours.

*M*oney without fun
is no fun.

*L*isten for the messages.
Be alert.
Be deliberately waiting.

*Y*ou cannot do it wrong,
only better and better.

Always do your best, for
your best is more
than enough.

Beauty is nature;
nature is God.
When you love nature
you love God.

Your outer world is a reflection of your inner life. Empty your mind of fear, hatred and guilt. Fill it with peace, joy and love.

Start each day with clear intent. Feel peace and love all day.

*T*rust your intuition.
The more you use it,
the more accurate
you become.

*L*et go of judgments.
They take you away from
compassion and lead
you to ego.

*L*ife continuously
sends you teachers,
each more intense than
the other, until you
learn the lesson.

*S*top complaining,
blaming and criticizing
your parents,
siblings and spouse.
Learn the lessons why you
chose this family and
move on.

*T*he ultimate goal of life
is understanding love.

$\mathcal{D}$esign your life
so nothing, no one,
interferes with your values.

$\mathcal{S}$eek a higher quality of
life. Stop thinking.

*H*onor your sacred spirit.
Live your life profoundly.

*F*ocus on the present, not
the past or the future.
Your heart's desires
will come true.

*L*isten with
an empty mind.
Respond with a full heart.

*T*hings happen
for a reason.
Trust that and move on.

*A*llow yourself to be human. Ask for the help you need to grow.

*I*nner peace and well-being flow from love and harmony, not from money and worldly power.

*F*eel the truth.
Send it love.

*S*urrender to the
perfection of the present.

*E*very time you hold back
what you feel, you
lose your personal power
and diminish your soul.

*F*ocus on the present and
the future will take
care of itself.

The present is perfect,
even when it seems
otherwise.

Everything is part of
what needs to happen
right now.

*S*tay focused on now.
Good things will
flow to you.

*B*e willing.
Be open.
Be still.

*T*hink it!

Feel it!

Materialize it!

*M*oney can be replaced,
a soul cannot.
Be willing to walk away.

*F*ully express what you
need and feel.
Let your spirit soar.

*W*hen your body speaks,
know there is
spiritual distress.

*S*uccess is feeling,
knowing and acting
simultaneously.

*H*ave clear intent before
beginning each and every
activity. Know that or
something better
will materialize.

$\mathcal{S}$uccess is
internally realized,
not externally achieved.

$\mathcal{C}$ome to God often.
Come to God with
an empty mind.
Come to God with
an open mind.

*R*eal power resides
in spiritual consciousness,
not material existence.

*S*uffering is your soul's
universal wake-up call
that you've
stepped off your path.

*I*f you are struggling and
trying hard, it's time to ask:
"What's wrong with
this picture?"

*S*top trying to fix, change
or improve anyone.
Raise your standards,
upgrade your friends.

*T*rust yourself
and your sensibilities –
physical and non-physical.
Embrace your authentic power.

*R*eal truth is felt internally,
not sensed externally.

Expand your
spiritual insight.
See the symbolic truths,
not just the literal
situations and events.

Vision becomes reality
when you take
responsibility and
accountability for
making it so.

Still your body,
quiet your mind, listen.

Trust yourself and God.
The right words will be there
at the right time.

*S*ay what you want to say,
not what you think others
want to hear.

*B*uild a community which
honors your gifts.

Deepen your awareness.
Keep an open attitude and
a listening ear.

Stop sabotaging yourself.
Act on your inner reality,
not the outer illusion.

$\mathcal{I}$ncrease
your consciousness.
See the symbolic
messages of life,
not the literal illusions,
that the Universe is
sending you.

$\mathcal{B}$e persistent.
Focus on the process,
not the results.

$\mathcal{L}$ove yourself enough
to take great care
of yourself.

*A*ll you seek is already
within you. You simply
need to ask.

*R*enew your energy.
Come from joy, peace
and love in all your
thoughts and actions.

*S*top anticipating.
Take the action,
have the conversation.
Feel your energy grow.

*E*liminate the situations,
people and practices that
drain your positive energy
and personal power.

See and accept the truth.
Release all negative
attitudes, memories
and beliefs.
Become your light self.

Be fearless. Know that
God has paved your path
ahead and left her
beneficent energy behind.

*F*ear saps the energy
of life.

*B*e at peace
where you are.
Allow the future to
materialize.

Be grateful. Focus your energies on all that you have, not on all that is missing from your life.

The only thing that gets in the way of your greatness is you.

*K*now that you are great.
You are a child of God.

*W*hen you have a great
relationship with yourself,
you have great
relationships with others.

$\mathcal{S}$ay no to anyone or anything that does not bring you unconditional happiness.

$\mathcal{H}$appiness is an internal attitude and responsibility.

The path to perfect health
is full expression.
No holdbacks.

Increase your level
of health, wealth and
happiness.
Let go of who and what
no longer works.

Your undigested thoughts, words and feelings eat you up mentally, physically and spiritually.

Allow time for the unexpected. Underpromise and overdeliver.

*T*rust your higher source.
Stop second-guessing
yourself.

*I*ntegrity is aligning
yourself with God's will.

*S*ay yes to your soul.
Say yes to your destiny.

*W*alk away from people
who want to fix you rather
than love you.

*L*et go of your armor.
Your angels will
protect you.

*T*here are no limitations,
only limiting perspectives.
Expand your view.

*L*et love be your armor.

*D*o the most loving things
you can for yourself.

$\mathscr{P}$ut your faith in love,
not fear and control.

$\mathscr{B}$e loved unconditionally
for who you are,
not what you do.

*L*isten and observe more.
Speak less.

*P*eople either work or
they don't. Be willing to
accept them, love them
and let them go.

Your needs are musts,
not options.

Stop sabotaging your
personal success.
Take care of your needs
first, not eventually.

*B*e self-fulfilling.
Put your needs 100 percent
ahead of anything
and anyone else.

*A*sk for assistance and
be grateful for growth.

$\mathcal{B}$e outrageous.
Say yes to your soul.

$\mathcal{B}$e at peace with
everyone and everything;
be at peace with yourself.

Be at peace.
Love yourself and others
unconditionally.

See and feel the perfection
in everyone and everything.
Send them love.

*E*veryone who
crosses your path
is there for a reason.
Live by this truth
and prosper.

*H*onor your higher self.
Embrace your feelings,
embrace your
personal power.

*E*xpress your
personal power.
Promote your
personal health –
physically, mentally,
spiritually.

*T*he present is perfect
when you come from love.

*B*eing responsible doesn't
mean taking ownership for
everyone and everything.

*H*ave more than
enough of everything.
Have a reserve.

*B*e willing to go to the
next level. Confront what
you most resist.

Love is the language
of abundance.

The more you focus on
the now, the more good
things will flow to you.

*R*elax and let go to
receive and achieve.

*I*t is time to stop making
things happen and allow
them to happen.

Stay active.
Keep focused.

Stop anticipating.
Show up.

*D*istinguish adrenaline
from energy. Move forward
naturally and easily.
Connect with your higher self.

*L*et go, clean up
everyone and everything
that is holding you back
from being complete.
Be in integrity.

$\mathcal{L}$isten to your heart.
Stop analyzing, criticizing
and trying to understand.

$\mathcal{B}$e selfish enough to be
self-fulfilling.

Connect with others.
Be them; feel them.

Look beyond to a deeper
level. See the beauty.
Send it love.

*W*hat you believe is
what you receive.
Be aware of what you
think and say.

*L*ife will change
when you do.
Give yourself permission.

Change
your surroundings;
open up your creativity.
Let your natural gifts flow.

Create the space that
works best for you.

$\mathcal{M}$ind-talk stops when
you fully communicate.

$\mathcal{B}$e detached. Say it all,
say it now — regardless.

*R*equest more than you
think you can or should.

*E*mbrace
your authentic power.
Speak from your heart,
not your head.

$\mathcal{O}$nly spend time with
people, places and things
that you love.

$\mathcal{C}$ome out of the fog.
Clear the clutter and
unfinished business
in your life.

*L*isten mindfully.
Act urgently.

*C*reativity flows when
you are having fun.
Give yourself permission
to pause, rest and play.
There is more than
enough time.

*B*e curious.
Be inspired all the time.

*B*e curious, not critical.

*O*bserve the world with
childlike curiosity.

*B*e detached.
Speak freely, express
your authentic power.

Turn inside.
There are no problems,
only solutions.
Allow the right next steps
to move you forward.

Choose God's will,
not yours. Act on faith,
love and integrity.

*T*he less you tolerate,
the brighter you shine.

*W*hen you are ready,
you will fly. Be patient.

*R*eceive God's truth and
speak it confidently.

*T*hought precedes form.
Be mindful of what
you think.

$\mathcal{T}$rust your inner guidance. Welcome divine wisdom to merge with your reasoning.

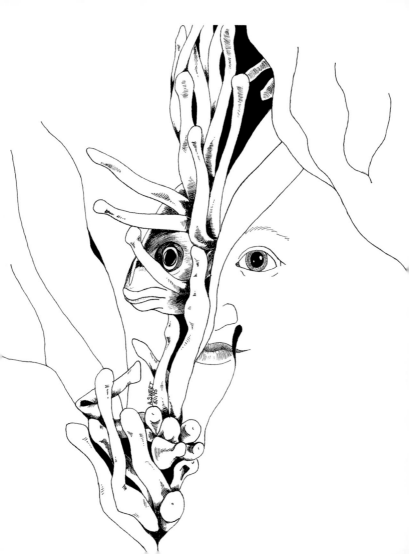

$\mathcal{L}$isten to your soul,
not your ego.

$\mathcal{W}$hen you hear that little
voice inside, know it's
your soul and honor it.

*B*e passionate.
Speak from your heart,
not your head.

*T*ell people what
you need.
Don't lose sight.
Don't lose heart.

*S*top tolerating.
Start communicating.
Start energizing.

*W*alk away from people
who want to discuss you
rather than accept you.

*T*rusting is knowing.

*S*ee it all.
See it for what it is.

*S*tay open and neutral.
Be in direct contact
with God.

*T*he key to having money
is your willingness
to receive it.

*B*e at cause for yourself;
not at the effect of
circumstances.

*L*et go of your external
dream; create your
internal reality.

Be responsible for your feelings, not others.

It is.

Greet each hour of each
day with curiosity.
Be grateful.

Stop analyzing it.
Accept it and move on.

*L*ive your life as if you
already were what
you believe.

*D*ivine guidance is
waiting. Quiet your mind.
Feel her presence.
Listen to her speak.
Take the action.

*F*ear is fabrication.

*R*elease your fear.
Critical judgment of
yourself and others creates
negative consequences —
physically, mentally,
and spiritually.

$\mathcal{L}$et go of fear.
Allow God's energy to
flow through you.

$\mathcal{B}$e like the bamboo tree.
No matter what life sends
you, stay centered and
flow with the wind.

*G*reatness is your
birthright.
You just need to
believe.

*I*t's never about others
liking you; it's about you
liking them.

*Y*our emotional health,
past and present, is your
physical health today.

*P*ersonal power is your
foundation of health.
Be in balance with your body,
mind and soul.

*N*urture yourself well.
Treat yourself better
than anyone else.
Be self-full!

*E*verything is possible.
God knows. Listen to
your inner voice.

The Universe
wants you to be
successful, joyous, happy.
Honor its messages.

Internal prompts are like
green lights and external
prompts are like red lights.
Embrace your green lights
and act on them now.

*S*urrender to your soul,
not circumstances.

*B*e in integrity.
Eliminate all the attitudes,
behaviors and acts
that do not honor your
divine greatness.

There are no accidents,
only lessons
and opportunities.

Life sends you lessons,
not enemies. Distinguish
the *what* from the *who*
and complete the lesson.

*G*o for life, not for living.

*L*ive your life
as if you already were
what you believe.

*B*e strong.
Fill your life with positive
thoughts, feelings, words
and actions.

*L*ife is not about making
others happy. Life is about
making you happy.
Others will benefit too.

While your eyes see
limits, your heart knows
no boundaries.
Trust your heart.
Expand your vision.

Come from love in all
that you think and do.
Express your God self.

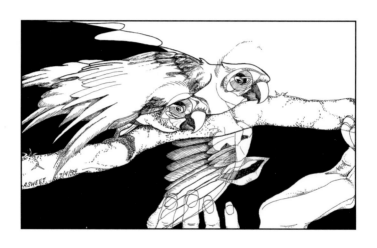

*L*ife mirrors
your perception.
Expand your vision.
Sharpen your focus.

$\mathcal{B}$e patient.
Peace and fulfillment
come in God's time
not yours.

$\mathcal{F}$ocus on what
brings utter peace and joy
to you and others.

*D*oing the "right" thing
brings acceptance. Being
your true self brings
inner peace and joy.

*W*hat you perceive is
what you receive.
Make it love.

$\mathcal{L}$earn the *what*,
not the *who*,
that saps your power.

$\mathcal{O}$wn your power.
Accept responsibility for
creating your life.
If it is not working,
take action for
re-creating it. Now.

$\mathcal{P}$lan to
carry out
your intention.

$\mathcal{T}$rust your feelings.
Honor your soul.

$\mathcal{L}$ess is more.

$\mathcal{S}$uccess is like riding
a roller coaster until you
have mastered life.

Give yourself permission
to be successful.
Listen to your heart
and take the action.

It's time to raise
your standards —
upgrade your beliefs,
friends, procedures
and actions.

$\mathcal{D}$o not despair
in your travesty.
Use it to catapult yourself
to the next level.

$\mathcal{I}$f you are struggling,
you are in the
wrong place.

$\mathcal{L}$et go of anyone and
anything that is more
struggle than ease.

$\mathcal{S}$urrender
to your inner voice.

$\mathcal{B}$e willing to let go of
anything and anyone who
is holding you back
from being all you
are meant to be.

$\mathcal{T}$here is a direct correlation
between your energy level
and degree of toleration.

*P*ause.
Enjoy the richness
of the moment.

*L*et go
of understanding *why*
things are the way
they are.

*A*s your soul grows
your ego shrinks,
naturally.

*T*here is wisdom in
nothingness.

$\mathscr{Y}$ou are
more than enough.
You do not need to prove
yourself anymore.

$\mathscr{F}$ear constricts the
pipeline of abundance.

*D*oors open
when you stop controlling
and start flowing.
Don't ask why.

*E*xpress your deepest
wants, desires and beliefs.

Be whole.
Take the action.
Have the conversation.

Don't pursue you;
be you.

*S*urround yourself with
the people, places and
activities that
bring you bliss.

*E*verything you
need and want is coming.
Know. Trust. Believe.

Give the message,
not the story.

Speak what is on your
mind and in your heart.

*S*uccess flows from
clear intent.

*P*lay to win.
Stop trying not to lose.

$\mathscr{S}$oulful inspiration is an
acquired habit.

$\mathscr{C}$ommitting to integrity
does not mean that you are
out of the storm, but that
you are learning how to
weather the storm.

$\mathcal{B}$e fully present.
Heighten your awareness
of the opportunities
all around you.

$\mathcal{L}$ife is meant to flow
effortlessly. Listen and act
on God's will,
not yours.

*D*etachment
is the path of truth.

*I*t's in the resisting
that we get tired.
Be willing to walk away
from who and what
is not working.

*C*alm yourself
with peaceful sounds.

*F*lowing is effortless.
Make decisions based on
values, not needs.

*T*he more you push,
the greater the resistance.
Stop pushing;
start flowing.

Stop trying to make
things happen that aren't
meant to happen.

Allow yourself to move
forward with ease.
Stop fighting to
maintain the status quo.

*T*here is no clarity
with clutter.

*I*ncompletions in life are
like boulders in the river.
They break
the river's power and
disperse its flow.

Only through forgiveness,
for yourself and others,
can you be all you are
meant to be.

Stop beating up on
yourself. Recognize that
you are doing
your best.

What I want for you is
a life of peace, joy and
prosperity.
Allow your natural gifts to
provide for you and others.

Appreciate today.

*I*ntegrity is being
responsible for our
actions and inactions.

*S*tand in integrity,
not righteousness.
Everything and everyone
you need to fulfill your
purpose will flow to you.

*H*andle your
external world.
Don't get caught up in it.

*Y*our first impression is
the right impression.
Trust.

Eliminate
the sugar-coating of life.
Enjoy life's natural
sweetness.

Stop doing you, be you.
Honor your sacredness.

*E*verything is possible
when you allow yourself
to say YES.

*E*mbrace
your authentic power.
Stand up for what
you believe —
regardless.

Stay on purpose
for yourself;
eliminate
the distractions.

Your reality
will change
when you change.

*Y*our thoughts and beliefs
shape your reality.
Make them positive.

*Y*ou create
your own reality.
Be aware of what you
think and say.

$\mathcal{R}$eserve is
having more
than enough for
the unexpected.

$\mathcal{E}$verything is a
part of what needs
to happen right now.

*B*e patient and
disciplined.
Things happen in
God's time, not yours.

*S*top tolerating limiting
thoughts from yourself
and others.

*S*tart creating behaviors, attitudes and situations that increase your energy and power.

*T*rust the irrational. Don't question or ask why. Listen and act on your inner voice.

Trust yourself before others.

There are no victims,
only lessons.

*L*ife doesn't need to be
one accident after another;
it's your choice.

*G*et unstuck. Stop
analyzing, questioning
and wondering.

*D*o your best every day.
The Universe
will support you.

*L*ook beyond the storm.
Get the message.
Be grateful.

Your future is cast by the
choices you make today.
Choose wisely.

Lessons from the past
will be clear when
you are ready.

*Y*our thoughts and words
shape your reality.
You can have it
any way you want.

*T*ell people what you
want. Most will say yes.
Some will negotiate.

Be selective where and with whom you spend your time.

It's not the number of relationships you have that counts, but how deep you go with them.

*L*isten.
Hear the message.
Take the action.
Now.

*B*uild the community
that you want.

*B*e committed to your
God-given gifts.

Balance your mind,
body and soul.
Take time to nurture
yourself.

Heighten your awareness
of the subtle tolerations
that drain you
physically, emotionally
and spiritually.

There are no failures;
there are only
golden seeds
of opportunities.

Fear is an illusion.
Put your faith
in truth and love.

*F*ear is like a dam
holding back
the river of life.
Release judgment, doubt
and disbelief. Open the
floodgates to prosperity.

*S*urrender fear, control,
attachments.
Know God walks
with you.

Change is natural.
Shift your fear of
the unknown
to knowing that all things
happen for divine reason.
Embrace the opportunity.

Feel it. Do it. Say it.
Now.

*H*eaven on Earth is now.

*F*ocus on those things
that nurture your soul
and feed your spirit.

*F*ocus on the now.
The future will show up
better than you planned.

*H*eal yourself
through acts of love,
forgiveness and faith.
Breathe God's
divine energy.

*P*ossibilities are probabilities fueled by desire and action.

*I*ntegrity is the key to all you are and all you achieve.

$\mathcal{B}$e committed to a
higher purpose.
Create your legacy.

$\mathcal{L}$et go of anyone and
anything that is more
work than play.

*L*ife is about showing up,
not anticipating.

*B*e a listener.
Hear it all. Say less.

$\mathcal{L}$ove yourself
enough to be No. 1.

$\mathcal{E}$verything you need
and want is here.
Set your sights higher.

*B*e positive.
Only do things you love.

*T*here are no accidents,
only possibilities.

*R*aise your standards.
Tell others how you want
to be treated.
Allow nothing less.

*R*eceiving is easy.
Provide exceptional service.
Meet others' needs,
not yours.

$\mathcal{B}$e responsible for your
feelings, not others.

$\mathcal{T}$here is only goodness.
All else is misperception.
Expand your view.

$\mathcal{P}$ut yourself in another's place. Then speak the truth confidently with compassion and love.

$\mathcal{Y}$ou can have anything you want. Surrender to the possibilities.

*W*hen you trust yourself,
you trust God.
Know God will never
mislead you.

*W*hen your mind feels
foggy, ask:
"What am I tolerating?"

*Today's truth
can change tomorrow.
Be willing to shift.*

*Align your
personal and professional
goals with your values.*

*S*top asking why.
Everything happens
for a reason.

*A*s you think,
so it will be.

*E*xpand your beliefs,
expand your joy and
happiness level.

*A*ctualize the riches and
richness of life.
Visualize the possibilities.

*A*cknowledge
your greatness.
Follow your heart.

*H*onor your inner voice.
It is sacred.

*A*cknowledge
and give thanks
for all that you have
and all you are.

A.SWEET 9/5/94

$\mathcal{G}$o forth knowing
that you are one
with God.
Everything is possible.

$\mathcal{U}$nleash your power.
Live fully in the present.
Stop reliving the past or
anticipating the future.

$\mathcal{B}$e conscious
of your needs.
Make requests.
Ask for answers.

$\mathcal{Y}$our external world is
a reflection of your
inner reality.
Clean up your space.

$\mathcal{B}$e at peace.
Still your mind. Go inside.
Feel God's presence —
strong, warm and confident.

$\mathcal{T}$ake time out to pamper
yourself daily, weekly,
monthly, quarterly
and annually.

$\mathcal{L}$ook for, recognize and acknowledge your own and others' magnificence.

$\mathcal{C}$are for your spirit as consciously as you care for your physical body.

*Y*ou are your priorities.

*R*isk dropping your
veil of perfection.
Be the gift you are.

*R*eclaim your
personal power.
Tell the truth.

*G*ive yourself permission
to think the unthinkable.
Honor your soul.
Honor your destiny.

*S*ynchronicity is your
natural state.

*B*e at one with God.
Be at peace.

More  ESSAGES from God

IF THESE MESSAGES HAVE TOUCHED your heart, awakened your spirit and changed your life, I would be honored to hear from you.

Special collections of *Messages From God* books are being planned for singles, parents, women, athletes, teenagers and business, among others. Your contributions to any of these volumes are welcomed.

Please submit any of the following:

◆ Your favorite motivational quotation or passage.

◆ An inspirational story that you may

have clipped out of the newspaper, a magazine or a company newsletter that touched you deeply.

◆ A *Messages from God* quote that spoke to your soul and inspired you to change your life. Share the message(s) and your personal experience.

Just send a copy of your stories and any other messages that have moved you to new levels in your life to:

Messages from God
P.O. Box 22545
Houston, TX 77227
Fax: 713-623-0135
www.lynnmarks.com
e-mail:info@lynnmarks.com

Both you and the author will be credited for your submission.

Love and warmest regards. — Lynn

$\mathcal{S}$UPPORTING
God's Children

IN THE SPIRIT OF SUPPORTING THE PRESENT so that the future will continue to be filled with limitless possibilities, I am donating a portion of the proceeds from *Messages from God: 365 Simple Truths for Success* to the following non-profit charity:

Big Brothers Big Sisters of America makes a positive difference in the lives of children and youth, primarily through a professionally supported One-To-One relationship with a caring adult, and to assist them in achieving their highest potential as they grow to become confident, competent and caring individuals.

To learn how you can make a positive impact in the life of a child, contact them at:

Big Brothers Big Sisters of America
230 North 13th Street
Philadelphia, PA 19107
215-567-7000
www.bbbsa.org

SPEAKING, RETREATS, AND COACHING

If you want more information about Lynn's services, including:

◆ seminars
◆ retreats
◆ personal coaching
◆ keynote speaking
◆ executive roundtables
◆ other products

please contact her at:
LYNN S. MARKS
P.O. Box 22545
Houston, TX 77227
Phone: 1-888-LYNN-321
Fax: 713-623-0135
or visit: www.lynnmarks.com

Who is Lynn?

LYNN S. MARKS IS REFOCUSING THE vision of what is possible in our lives. A professional speaker on personal power and spirituality, she is a pioneer in the field of business coaching. Lynn has an infectious spirit and ability to help others reach their full potential. She coaches entrepreneurs, professionals and private individuals on their career and lives. Lynn informs and inspires audiences and clients alike to reach new levels of self-confidence, peak performance and personal success. Widely sought out for her wisdom, Lynn has more than 25 years experience in management, education, public relations and organizational change.

ℐHARE THE MAGIC OF
ℳESSAGES from God™
365 Simple Truths for Success

A collection of 365 messages of wisdom. Whether you buy it for yourself or as a gift for others, it's sure to open your heart, awaken your spirit and change your life.

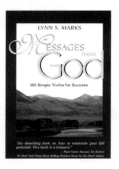

Code MFG01 Hardback $14.95

Available at your favorite bookstore.

To order other products:
Please use the enclosed card or visit our website at: www.lynnmarks.com

Prices do not include shipping or handling.

More Magic from

ℳ̲ESSAGES from God™
365 Simple Truths for Success

Inspirational Posters

Take yourself, your family, your business to the next level. These posters feature inspirational messages from the best-selling *Messages from God*. And, remember your community. They make welcomed gifts for family, friends and colleagues.

Each 11" x 17" unframed poster is on high-quality, designer paper.

Code	Title	Price
P01	Messages from God to Awaken Spirit	$20.00
P02	Messages from God to Awaken Love	$20.00
P03	Messages from God to Awaken Inner Wisdom	$20.00
P04	Messages from God to Awaken Personal Power	$20.00
P05	Messages from God to Awaken Leadership	$20.00
P06	Messages from God to Awaken Peace	$20.00
P07	Messages from God to Awaken Attitude	$20.00
P08	Messages from God to Awaken Self-Esteem	$20.00

To order these products:
Please use the enclosed card or visit our website at: www.lynnmarks.com

Prices do not include shipping or handling.

LYNN'S INSPIRATIONAL TAPES
Strategies for Your Personal Success

With warmth and clarity, Lynn empowers you to create the life you really want — now! By following the wisdom outlined in these seven key strategies, your life — personally and professionally — will shift to one of productivity, prosperity and peace.

Code PSA one 65-minute audiocassette $12.00
Code PSV one 65-minute videocassette $39.00

A GIFT OF INSPIRATION AND LOVE
Your Path to Success

Inspire your life or your friends with a gift of faith, love and inspiration. Purple 100% pre-shrunk cotton T-shirt with *Messages from God*™ puff-designed graphic and message on back in gold and white and Friends of Lynn logo on front pocket area. Available only XL.

Code T002 T-shirt $20.00

To order these products:
Please use the enclosed card or visit our website at: www.lynnmarks.com

Prices do not include shipping or handling.

Power of the Self
Inspirational Tape Series

Whether you are a corporate executive, business owner, sales manager or parent, you need *Power of the Self.*

Loaded with empowerment strategies, anecdotal success stories and spiritual wisdom, you'll learn valuable insights that will take you — personally and professionally — to the next level.

Be empowered by Lynn's warmth, energy and inspirational *"Messages from God."* Gain the enthusiasm and reward of a positive life as you cultivate love, joy, faith, integrity and fulfillment.

Recorded live at Lynn's monthly luncheon, this series includes 12 universal messages for daily inspiration and success.

Code PSS	**Power of the Self**	**$79.00**
	6-Tape Album	

To order this item:
Please use the enclosed card or visit our website at: www.lynnmarks.com

Prices do not include shipping or handling.